AC

The author wishes to thank the

Dr. Jon Springer for his inspiration and guidance throughout this project, without his introduction to Memetics, this paper would not have been possible.

Dr. Henry Kaplowitz for his support and guidance as my program coordinator.

My girlfriend Mary, for her constant support and guidance as well as putting up with many nights of discussions relating to suicide bombers.

My family for their support throughout my life.

All of my past, present and future educators who have allowed me to get to where I am today.

I thank you all from the bottom of my heart.

CHAPTER 1

THE BASICS OF SUICIDE BOMBINGS

The questions of interest include the following: The seeming correlation, loosely defined, between high youth populations, environmental challenging conditions, higher total fertility rates, perceived inequities and injustices (religious outrage over infidels) and the presence of a culturally appropriate (Memetic) means of redress of suicide bombings. Additionally, explaining how suicide bombings may include a partial interpretation of the evolutionary psychology concepts of the *inclusive fitness*, *parental investment* and reported altruistic responses by suicide bombers. A meaningful evolutionary psychological profile and explanation is thus possible for past, present and potential suicide bombers. In addition to the above questions, it is further proposed that explanations of suicide bombing would include how this is linked through memetic culture (memeplex) of religion, itself a meme as well as other memes such as the "terrorist meme".

Involved Factors

A comparison of the typical ages of potential suicide bombers (the study's population) is required in order to evaluate the high youth populations in various countries. In the United States, the Total Fertility Rate[1] (TFR) is 2.1. When looking

---

[1] (TFR): The average number of children that would be born to a woman over her lifetime if she were to experience the current age-specific fertility rates through her lifetime.

at the countries that have a large number of suicide bombing incidents, the TFR's range from 4.2 in Iraq to 7.1 in Yemen which is significantly higher than that in the United States and the other 79 developed nations. But what does this mean? When the TFR exceeds what is considered the replenishment rate the country is left with a critical youth bulge (ages 1529) in population.

According to Triver's (1972) theory of *parental investment*[2], parents have a limited number of available financial and time resources. In order to ensure the survival of their offspring, a certain amount of time is required per offspring. Those offspring that have the highest chance at survival will usually receive the largest amount of investment as they are most likely to produce offspring of their own and continue the family blood line. On the converse side, those that have the least chance at survival, i.e. newborns and defective youngest children, will have a lesser opportunity for the available resources. In a country such as the United States where the TFR is 2.1, the resources available only need to be divided between two offspring so the likelihood of survival increases. However, in a country such as Yemen with a TFR of 7.1, the limited resources must be divided among potentially seven children. This limitation on resources for the vulnerable youth population, in conjunction with environmental challenges sets the stage for suicide terrorism.

---

[2] Parental investment (PI) refers to a concept in evolutionary ecology defined as any parental expenditure (time, energy etc.) that benefits one offspring at a cost to parents' ability to invest in other components of fitness. Components of fitness include the wellbeing of existing offspring, parents' future reproduction, and inclusive fitness through aid to kin.

Thus the environmental factors and economic depression may provide conditions in which parents may choose to sacrifice their younger children, to training camps for suicide bombers, in exchange for large cash awards and social status upgrades.

The ultimate goal of organisms to have the maximum number of offspring possible to continue their genetic contributions within the population. This was the position taken in R. Dawkins (1976) classical and seminal work *The Selfish Gene*. Also to be taken into account, are the factors associated with the inclusive fitness. Hamilton's theory of inclusive fitness[3] (1964) includes the core ideas behind Darwin's Fitness theory as well as behaviors that aid an organism's individual fitness through the use of altruism[4]. Triver's (1972) hypothesis Parental Investment states that while attempting to maintain the highest number of offspring, the resources must allocated, and occasionally an offspring must be sacrificed for the greater good. In some species (for example, ospreys) the parent(s) will murder their weakest and least fit of the offspring and in some species it is almost always the second born of the two.

Some Definitions

---

[3] Inclusive Fitness (IF): encompasses conventional Darwinian fitness with the addition of behaviors that contribute to an organism's individual fitness through altruism. An organism's ultimate goal is to leave the maximum number of viable offspring possible, thereby keeping their genes present within a population.

[4] Altruism: The practice of placing others before oneself

In order to understand Suicide Bombings, we must first clarify what it is. Many definitions have been produced ranging from the international arena, to the military, and even coming from the religious sector. According to the religious sector, "a suicide bombing is usually that the participant wires themselves up, or a vehicle or suitcase, with explosives, and then tries to enter amongst a conglomeration of the enemy, or in their vital facilities, and to detonate in an appropriate place there in order to cause the maximum looses in the enemy rank, taking advantage of the element of surprise and penetration. The participant of the operation guarantees themselves absolute death by detonating the bomb with their own hands, in a genuine suicide mission" (The Hijacked Caravan, 2006). In the international arena, suicide bombings aren't well defined. The closest working definition is an attack in which the attacker or attackers intend to kill others and intend to die in the process. In a suicide attack in the strict sense the attacker dies by the attack itself, for example in an explosion or crash caused by the attacker. While these definitions work to explain what constitutes terrorism, they fail to explain what is meant by Suicide Terrorism. Suicide Terrorism is defined as, "the targeted use of self-destructing humans against noncombatant, typically civilian, populations to effect political change" (Atran, 2003). While this is an effective definition, Bloom (2004) says that suicide bombings are violent, politically motivated attacks, carried out in a deliberate state of awareness by a person who blows himself/herself up together with a chosen target. These two operational definitions change in the respect that Atran suggests suicide bombers are only used against noncombatants, while Bloom suggests that there is no status associated with the victims of suicide attacks.

This operational definition is not that far off from the definition of terrorism as a whole. According to Atran (2003), Terrorism is defined as "premeditated, politically motivated violence perpetrated against noncombatant targets by subnational groups or clandestine agents, usually intended to influence an audience." This definition applies to statistical research and policy making.

On the other hand, Atran (2003) points out that Terrorism is "an activity that—(A) involves a violent act or an act dangerous to human life that is a violation of the criminal laws of the United States or any State, or that would be a criminal violation if committed within the jurisdiction of the United States or of any State; and (B) appears to be intended (i) to intimidate or coerce a civilian population; (ii) to influence the policy of a government by intimidation or coercion; or (iii) to affect the conduct of a government by assassination or kidnapping." This definition is used in determining criminal matters in the USA.

Therefore, suicide bombings fit nicely into the broad definition of terrorism in that it is an activity that is violent, dangerous to human life, and is usually unlawful according to the government in which the act occurs. The act itself is also premeditated, however not always politically motivated nor always against non-combatant targets with the intention to influence an audience. With this operational definition in mind, we may proceed to the explanation of the types of suicide bombings.

Types of Suicide Bombings

When most people think about suicide bombings, they recall what they heard on the radio or saw on the television set. The most traditional and sometimes easiest type of Suicide Bomb is the vest style bomb. This type of device allows the wearer to put on a vest laden with explosives, connected to some type of a trigger mechanism which will allow them to detonate the device at the appropriate time. The basic devices are sometimes complicated in that a remote is added to the device, allowing a user to remotely detonate the device in the event that the wearer is either unable to or unwilling to detonate the device. This type of addition would slightly change the parameters of a suicide bombing in that, the device wearer did not have control over when the device activated.

An additional feature that has been added to these devices is nicknamed "Dead Man's Triggers." These types of triggers work opposite that of a normal trigger. In a normal trigger, the plunger or button is depressed, creating a closed circuit, which then activates the device. When using a Dead Man's Trigger, the device plunger is depressed, at which time the device is armed. If the plunger is allowed to return to its normal non-depressed position, the device activates. This poses special hazards to anyone in the area in that, the wearer is still able to detonate the device when they choose to do so, and the traditional method of shooting the wearer to stop the bombing will prove fruitless.

Another type of Suicide Bomb is referred to as a Vehicle Borne Improvised Explosive Device (henceforth VBIED). These types of devices are essentially motor vehicles, cars or trucks, which are loaded with a large amount of explosives and driven into a location in order to destroy it. This type of device was seen as a Suicide Bombing in the attacks on the U.S. Marine Corp Barracks in Beirut, Lebanon in 1983. This was a major incident during the Lebanese Civil War. Two truck bombs struck buildings in Beirut housing U.S. and French members of the Multinational Force in Lebanon, killing hundreds of soldiers, the majority being U.S. Marines. The October 23, 1983, blasts led to the withdrawal of the international peacekeeping force from Lebanon, where they had been stationed since the Israeli invasion in 1982. The suicide bomber detonated his explosives, which were equivalent to 12,000 pounds of TNT[5]. The force of the explosion collapsed the four-story cinder-block building into rubble, crushing many inside. There were 299 soldiers, 6 civilians, and 2 suicide bombers killed in the attack, as well as 75 injuries.

Although not a suicide vehicle bomb, the device used by Timothy McVeigh in

---

[5] TNT- an explosive with the common designation *trinitrotoluene*. The explosive yield of TNT is considered the standard measure of strength of bombs and other explosives

the 1995 bombing of the Murray Federal Building in Oklahoma City, Oklahoma was a VBIED. McVeigh used a large box style truck, filled with a combination of Ammonium Nitrate and Fuel Oil mixture to destroy a large portion of the federal building and to murder 168 people.

These types of devices have been in widespread use for over forty years due to the destructive nature of the device. Below is a chart produced by the Bureau of Alcohol, Tobacco, and Firearms dealing with the amount of explosives and stand off distances for VBIEDs in order to give an understanding of how many pounds of explosives a terrorist can place into a vehicle.

BATF Explosive Standards

	Vehicle Description	Maximum Explosives Capacity	Lethal Air Blast Range	Minimum Evacuation Distance	Falling Glass Hazard
	Compact Sedan	500 pounds 227 Kilos (In Trunk)	100 Feet 30 Meters	1,500 Feet 457 Meters	1,250 Feet 381 Meters
	Full Size Sedan	1,000 Pounds 455 Kilos (In Trunk)	125 Feet 38 Meters	1,750 Feet 534 Meters	1,750 Feet 534 Meters
	Passenger Van or Cargo Van	4,000 Pounds 1,818 Kilos	200 Feet 61 Meters	2,750 Feet 838 Meters	2,750 Feet 838 Meters
	Small Box Van (14 Ft. box)	10,000 Pounds 4,545 Kilos	300 Feet 91 Meters	3,750 Feet 1,143 Meters	3,750 Feet 1,143 Meters
	Box Van or Water/Fuel Truck	30,000 Pounds 13,636 Kilos	450 Feet 137 Meters	6,500 Feet 1,982 Meters	6,500 Feet 1,982 Meters
	Semi-Trailer	60,000 Pounds 27,273 Kilos	600 Feet 183 Meters	7,000 Feet 2,134 Meters	7,000 Feet 2,134 Meters

Figure 1. BATF Table (Retrieved from http://www.atf.gov)

While there are other types of suicide bombs, the vest style and car or vehicle style bombs are the two most commonly used methods. Now that the types are understood, next we look at the investigation of suicide bombings.

CHAPTER 2

INVESTIGATING SUICIDE BOMBINGS

The problem under investigation is the continued and projected use of suicide bombers. There are a variety of factors that must be present in order to form a cache of suicide bombers.

What external influences must be present to aid in the formation of the suicide bombers' mentality? There are multiple external influences in one's decision to become a human bomb. The socioeconomic statuses of the family's of these human bombs are a prime factor in their determination to die for their cause. In the West Bank, Hamas has paid significant sums of money to the families of recruited suicide bombers. Payment as high as ten to twenty five thousand dollars (US currency) have been made to families that have a monthly income of a mere three-hundred and fifty two dollars (US currency). Other terrorist recruiting organizations have been known to make a one time payment in excess of twenty-five thousand dollars to the families of suicide bombing recruits. This monetary stipend is important to the families in order to ensure the survival of their remaining children and themselves.

It has been said that poverty plays a vital role in terrorism. Krueger & Maleckova (2003) point out that there is little direct connection between poverty and terrorism. In support of this is that Palestinian suicide bombers are at least as likely to come from upper class homes as they are from lower class homes. According to Krueger & Maleckova (2002), in March 2002, Iraq had increased the one time payment made to the families of suicide bombings from $10,000 to $25,000 dollars. The month of April had a dramatic rise in the number of suicide bombings, although there is no evidence of a direct connection. While there may have been a correlation between the increase in the one time payment to the families of suicide bombers and the rise in the number of bombings, there is no direct causality. This does, however, demonstrate that there is a strong financial motive behind the convincing of a candidate to become a human bomb.

According to the Palestinian Central Bureau of Statistics, the poverty rate in the West Bank is 14.5% with a Fertility Rate of 5.44. The Gaza Strip has a 33.0% poverty rate with a Fertility Rate of 7.41. With a poverty rate of one in three people, a large cash influx would allow that particular family to move up and out of the poverty level, and into a more socially acceptable way of life.

Evolutionary Aspects

According to Blackwell (2005), the relative cost of parental investment needed to raise a child to maturity will be greater for poorer individuals. Therefore, the altruism exhibited by suicide bomber candidates to support their families is a strong influence on their decisions. For what these candidates could not provide in life, they will be providing for their families after their death. When this decision making process gets clouded, is when looking at the poorest of the poor members of the population. While sacrificing oneself may yield a high payment to the family and the potential to improve the family's status, losing a vital member of the family will result in a negative aspect, one that a large cash payment will not be able to overcome when compared to the potential earnings of that individual in the next few years.

Also, in terms of associated costs, Blackwell (2005) points out that 84% of Palestinian attackers are unmarried, and 99% of them are male. He further explains how this is directly attributable to the potential mating opportunities or lack thereof available to the candidate.

In an environment where there is an uneven sex ratio and polygamy opportunities, the availability of mates is most commonly correlated with social and economic factors. A suicide bomber candidate, coming from a relatively poor family, may not be able to acquire a suitable mate due to their lack of financial status. However, through their sacrifice, the remaining members of their family will be provided with the financial support and status to obtain an appropriate mate. The other major selection process in mating is that a large number of marriages (48%) are between relatives, usually cousins. This limits the appropriate number of potential mates and increases the competition for marriage partners. This limitation on mating allows for a higher degree of relatedness between the families. This higher degree of relatedness and the overall malnutrition rates combined with infant mortality rates provide a substantial economic benefit associated with these fitness effects. (Blackwell 2005)

Blackwell (2005) shows how 81% of suicide bombers come from families with at least eight members including six or more siblings. This family size is larger than the mean household of seven members. This altruistic response allows the honor and status of a suicide bomber to be transferred to their family thus increasing the likelihood of potential mates and monetary support.

What could be a potential motivation to strap explosives to your chest and end your life? In a study by Kruglanski & Golec (2004), Individual motivations were assessed. It was discovered that on an individual level there are two major factors associated with suicide bombers. First, there is the assertion of autonomy. Large portions of suicide bombers are between the ages of eighteen and twenty-seven during which there are biological changes, the development of high quantities of testosterone, and increased educational levels. These individuals wish to exert their newly found autonomy and often cannot due to their situation. This may lead to frustration and the need for control. These individuals seek out new leadership away from their parents and family structure and seek to find a new way of life. As the final steps to transitioning into adulthood are obtained, the individuals are prone to experimenting with different social roles, trying out new ways of thinking and behavior, and exploring new ideas.

There is also the idea of the assertion of significance. During the transition from childhood into adulthood, the individual may feel as though they have gone from being the "apple of their parents' eye" to being an insignificant individual in the world filled with adults. One example given is "a placement at the bottom of a heap in a hugely insignificant social position. (Kruglanski & Golec 2004 pg. 76)". This feeling of insignificance, combined with lack of ambition in life, or a misunderstanding of where the individual is expected to be in life, can lead to recruitment by suicide groups. These recruited individuals are impressionable, able-bodied, and under the direction of a "new family" structure accepting the roles to which they are assigned. Kruglanski & Golec (2004) state, "The attention-getting potential of a suicide is multiplied in the case of suicide terrorism where the would-be perpetrator can often expect considerable pomp and circumstance with which his death would be greeted. Add to it the 72 black-eyed virgins, a guaranteed place in heaven for one's family, as well as a generous earthly support to the tune of several thousands of dollars, [in the recent past provided to Palestinian suicide bombers by various sponsors such as the Iraqis or the Saudis] and the allure can be quite powerful (Kruglanski & Golec 2004 pg. 92)". All of these factors combined have been a great influence on younger individuals with strong religious beliefs to become suicide bombers.

Religious Aspects

What cultural or religious objectives must be met to induce or recruit an individual to become a suicide bomber? In order for an individual to become a potential suicide bomber, there are a number of religious and cultural objectives that must be met.

First, suicide by its very nature is against the Muslim religion. This will result in cognitive dissonance between the candidates religious beliefs and the perceived benefits associated with their act.

According to the Hadith[6], the technique of suicide bombings can be deemed suicidal and murderous acts within Islam and are forbidden. "Do not kill yourselves. Verily, Allah is Merciful to you. And, whoever does that, out of aggression and injustice. We shall burn him in a Fire. And that is easy for Allah (Holy Qur'an 4:29-30)." This is an example of the feared eternal damnation that will be received by the suicide bomber upon their death. Furthermore, "And spend of your substance in the cause of Allah, and make not your own hands

---

[6] Hadith- traditions relating to the words and deeds of Muhammad. Hadith collections are regarded as important tools for determining the Sunnah, or Muslim way of life, by all traditional schools of jurisprudence.

contribute to your destruction; but do good; for Allah loves those who do good (Holy Qur'an 2:195)." refers to the illegitimacy of suicide bombings as the warning is clear, not to contribute to your own death as most suicide bombers do when they press the detonator to trigger the bomb.

Moving along from the suicide aspect into the homicide aspect, the Qur'an points out, "So, We decreed for the tribe of Israel that if someone kills another person-unless it is in retaliation for someone else or for causing corruption in the earth- it is as if he had murdered all of mankind (5:32)." Murder is considered a heinous crime for Islam. The beliefs include terrible consequences in the next life and those who are human bombs, will kill civilians when they detonate their bomb.

There are different beliefs according to the Holy Qur'an when it comes to killing civilians, Muslims, Non-Muslims, Women and Children. In terms of killing Muslims, the Holy Qur'an states "As for anyone who kills a Mu'min[7] deliberately, his repayment is Hell, remaining in it timelessly, forever. Allah is angry with him and has cursed him, and has prepared from a terrible punishment (4:92). In the same vein, it was stated, "The cessation of the temporal world is less significant to Allah than the killing of a single Muslim person." Therefore any suicide bomber that deliberately kills a Muslim faces eternal damnation.

---

[7] Mu'min-Believing Muslim

In terms of killing a non-Muslim, "Whoever killed a person having a treaty with the Muslims shall not smell the fragrance of Paradise though its fragrance is perceived from a distance of forty years." (al-Bukhari[8]) If the individual killed is considered to be a protected person, either by treaty or dealings with the government, the consequences are severe. In terms of killing women and children, "The Prophet forbade the killing of women and children" (Malik[9]) There is an explicit injunction in the Qur'an that expressly forbids the killing of women, children, the sick, and religious devotees. If women are deployed into the war, she is usually in a support function and a non-combatant. Utilizing women and children in operations or targeting them or considering the collateral damage is forbidden by the Shari'ah[10]. (The Hijacked Caravan 2000).

Suicide bombers may be recruited under the guise that they are not committing suicide by carrying out their mission, yet they are becoming Martyrs in

---

[8] Al-Bukhari-or just Bukhari is an Arabic nesbat, meaning "from Bukhara", the old Persian location of what is today Uzbekistan. It is usually added at the end of names as a specifier. The most known Al-Bukhari is Muhammad Ibn Ismail al-Bukhari, the Sunni scholar.

[9] Malik- Anas ibn Malik ibn al-Nadr (d.ca. 709) was a well-known *sahabi* (companion) of the Prophet Muhammad. He had been presented to the Muhammad by his mother at an early age in fulfillment of a vow. After the Muhammad's death in 632 he participated in the wars of conquest. One hundred and twenty eight *ahadith* narrated on his authority are to be found in the collections of *Sahih Bukhari* and *Sahih Muslim*.

[10] Shari'ah- refers to the body of Islamic law. The term means "way" or "path"; it is the legal framework within which public and some private aspects of life are regulated for those living in a legal system based on Muslim principles of jurisprudence.

the war against the infidels[11]. By becoming a martyr, the candidate believes that they will have access to the riches of the heavens and all associated benefits. However, martyrs, like suicide bombers are disgraced individuals according to Islamic Law. According to The Hijacked Caravan, "The Martyred Islamic Warrior [Shaheed Mujahid[12]] is the one who is martyred during a martial Jihad[13], in distinction to the other types of Shaheed.

In order for the Mujahid to qualify as a Shaheed in the battlefield, he must fulfill two criteria; firstly, he must be killed by means or weapons other than his own; and secondly, he must not know the precise moment of his own death." Neither of

---

[11] Infidel-one who doubts or rejects central tenets of a religion, especially those regarding its deities. One who doubts or rejects a particular doctrine, system or principle. In Islam, the Arabic word *kafir* refers to non-Muslims, often in a derogatory sense, and is usually translated into English as "infidel" or "unbeliever".

[12] Shaheed Mujahid-Shaheed is a religious term in Islam, that literally means "witness". It is a title that is given to a Muslim after his death, if he died during fulfillment of a religious commandment, or during a war for the religion. After fulfilling their religious commandment, a Muslim is to receive 72 red headed virgins in heaven. Mujahid- is an Arabic term, literally translated means "struggler"

[13] Jihad- is often used to describe purely physical and military "religious war", through physical struggle. Muslim scholars say that this understanding only makes up part of the broader meaning of the concept of *jihad*. The denotation is of a struggle, challenge, difficulty or (frequently) opposed effort, made either in accomplishment or as resistance.

these criteria may be fulfilled by suicide bombers as they carry the weapon of their death, being the explosives, and know the precise moment of their death as the moment that they detonate the explosives. As such, the rewards promised to, and sought by the suicide bombing candidates will not be found in the afterlife according to Islamic Law, yet the "Fires of Allah" await them.

So, knowing that the rewards promised may not exist, what causes that recruited candidate to continue with their mission? The answer is purely rhetoric. The candidates are lead to believe that the interpretation of the Holy Qur'an do not specifically eliminate them as Martyrs, yet elevates their status to Martyrdom due to the perceive Jihad on the Infidels.

In a study done by Khashan (2003), it was proposed that Islamic militancy, poverty, youth and personality patterns contribute to the explanation of support for Palestinian suicide bombings, as well as proneness to participate in them. This study focused on a large group of Palestinian refugees living in Lebanon. A vast majority of this group believed in Political Islam. Political Islam plays an important role in the development of ideologies related to terrorism. This role when combined with provocation from an external source and frustration in general can lead to reasonable religious individuals leaning towards the violent side and becoming suicide bombers. The results of this study showed that when combined with strong religious beliefs, poverty can be the trigger that will cause refugees to become violent suicide bombers.

Religion plays an important role in the determination of suicide bombers. Schbley (1990) conducted interviews with twenty-six individuals who had been involved in the planning and execution of terrorist activities, most commonly hostage taking. These interviews revealed how religious terrorism, fighting for your religion, has been a major influence on suicide attacks. The following facts are excerpted from those interviews: 1.) all the interviewees indicated suicide missions are reserved for individuals without dependents for example: children. 2.) All the interviewees indicated their willingness to execute suicide missions. 3.) All the interviewees indicated that God is their witness; therefore, there is no need for news coverage. 4.) Most of the interviewees were not concerned with international opinion. What draws particular interest is point number three. All of the interviewees indicated that God is their witness; therefore, there is no need for news coverage. With that having been said, a strong link between religion and terrorism can be established, at least within this particular group.

Mumford (2004) illustrates how the lack of understanding of the reasons why someone would become a suicide bomber has brought the best and the brightest psychologists together to the American Psychological Associations group on determining how to contain the growth of suicide bombers. It is hard to fathom why any individual would go against the natural instinct of self-preservation however, through the research shown here, a number of ideas are presented.

Ratner (2004) attempts to illustrate the cultural perspective associated with terrorism. In his explanation, shame is created when a foreigner invades what is considered to be sacred to a resident. In the case of Fallajuh, a soldier entering the home of a native resident is considered a shame. Shame, as a cultural perspective, is held in high regard and must be avenged. The senior male of the household has the duty to act and to correct the shame. Until this shame has been corrected, the family must continue to fight. This explanation yields an interesting insight into cultural beliefs, such that the senior male of the house or a dependant child will attack the soldiers, thus committing suicide if necessary, to avenge the shame that was brought on their family.

Economic Costs

What are the economic costs and the environmental variables that cause an individual to sacrifice themselves to a terrorist recruiter? As previously discussed, the environmental factors and economic factors that involve a candidate's decision to sacrifice themselves to a terrorist recruiter are multiple. With a large population, and limited natural resources, someone is bound to be shorted or slighted. If, through the nature of their sacrifice, the candidate can provide for their family with monetary support, as well as the perceived guaranteed place in heaven, then that would alleviate their burden on their family and on the economy, while providing a substantially better lifestyle for their family members. When the mean family size is eight, living in a small, confined area, with limited resources that do not allow all of the family members to eat properly, the result is a large infant mortality rate and malnutrition rate. These rates, in combination with the feelings of being isolated and left out of the family, due to the lack of parental investment, provide a strong base for a candidate to seek a new family structure, while proving their worth to their biological family.

CHAPTER 3

TERRORISM RESEARCH

There has been a tremendous amount of research into the field of terrorism, particularly in the past few years with the events of September 11th, 2001. A large amount of research material was utilized to write this paper and the need to summarize it was great. Below is a history of the suicide attack as well as the trending of suicide bombings by a variety of national and sub national groups beginning many decades ago, and increasing in frequency and scope around the 1980's.

Suicide attacks, and in particular suicide bombings are not a new concept. Suicide attacks have been around for decades, often associated with World War II and the Japanese Kamikaze pilots. In the 1980's, the LTTE or Tamil Tigers of Sri Lanka have made suicide attacks a preferred method of operation as there is a low physical cost associated and the potential for casualties is huge. More recently, the world has seen suicide attacks in Iraq, Israel, Chechnya, Lebanon, the United States, Palestine, and other countries.

Asymmetric warfare[14] has been around for a number of years as well, and just recently began being referred to as synonymous with Terrorism. The use of

---

[14] Asymmetric Warfare- a term that describes a military situation in which two belligerents of unequal strength interact and take advantage of their respective strengths and weaknesses. This interaction often involves strategies and tactics outside the bounds of conventional warfare.

suicide bombings often results from an agency or party having very little power and it is used as a response method to the actions of another more powerful group. In recent world events, this may be seen in the Israel-Palestinian conflict, Iraq, and Al-Qaeda's fight against the United States. The first recorded suicide bombing was back in 1881 with the assassination of Czar Alexander II of Russia. Czar Alexander was killed by Ignacy Hryniewiecki when Ignacy detonated home made hand grenades near the Winter Palace, blowing up Czar Alexander II's vehicle. The Japanese used Kamikaze pilots, who flew their planes into targets, thus creating an explosive condition as well as the Kaiten.[15]

Beginning in the 1980's, the frequency and scope of suicide bombings increased as did the use of vehicle borne bombs, namely car and truck bombs. There were 42 reported car and truck bombings in the world during this period. The first suicide bombing of this period was in 1981, with the car bombing of the Iraqi embassy in Beirut, by the Islamic Dawa Party[16]. Following this was the 1983 bombing of the U.S. Embassy in April and the October bombing of the Marine Corp Barracks in Beirut which is rumored to have been perpetrated by Hezbollah but never confirmed. The Tamil Tigers, also known as the LTTE, perfected the tactic of suicide bombings and generated its interest in other groups in the world.

---

[15] Kaiten-one or two man piloted torpedoes

[16] Islamic Dawa Party-Islamic Call Party is a militant Shiite Islamic group.

Specifically, their Black Tiger unit[17] is responsible for a large number of suicide bombings. More than 270 Black Tigers have died in various bombings both on the open waters and on land. Their victims include Indian Prime Minister Rajiv Gandhi, assassinated on May 21, 1991 by a female suicide bomber and Sri Lankan President Ranasinghe Premadasa, assassinated on May 1, 1993 by a suicide bomber.

During the early 1990's, the IRA[18] recruited men to become drivers for vehicle bombs in attacks on the British Army. These men were often threatened with the deaths of their families if they did not comply. The IRA was not very big in the concept of Suicide Bombings, at least not as large into it as the Tamil Tigers. In the 1990s, there were 30 attacks involving car and truck bombs in 23 countries including both the Oklahoma City Bombing and the first World Trade Center attack. The following incidents are representative:

1) On February 26th, 1993 at approximately 12:17 p.m. a large bomb exploded within the confines of the parking structure of the North Tower in the World Trade Center complex. This detonation killed six people and injured 1,042. While

---

[17] Black Tiger Unit- special operatives of the LTTE that commit suicide if needed to reach their objectives. They are considered to be one of the most elite and lethal suicide bombers in the world.

[18] IRA-Irish Republican Army

the overall death toll wasn't high by any means, the original intent of the bomb was to collapse the foundation of the North Tower, and bring the North tower crashing into the South Tower, ultimately bringing both down to the ground. This attack failed in its scope, and was not a suicide bombing, but sets the stage for the events of September 11th, 2001 which utilized planes in suicide attacks. These planes ultimately completed the mission originally intended for February 26th, 1993.

2) On June 25th, 1996 The Khobar Towers, a housing complex in the city of Khobar were destroyed by a suicide car bombing. The towers were being used to house foreign military personnel, including Americans. Terrorists exploded a fuel truck adjacent to Building #131. In all, 20 individuals were killed and 372 were wounded.

3) On August 7th, 1998 257 people were killed and over 4,000 wounded in simultaneous suicide car bombings at the United States embassies in the East African capital cities of Dar es Salaam, Tanzania and Nairobi, Kenya. This attack, in conjunction with the Khobar Towers and the 2000 account on the USS Cole were the major incidents against the United States and its personnel nationwide, prior to September 11th, 2001.

4) On October 12th, 2000 while she was harbored in the Yemeni port of Aden the

USS *Cole* was attacked from a small boat by suicide bombers, Seventeen sailors were killed and 39 were injured. Although, the loss of life was minimal, the financial costs associated with the rescue and recovery of this ship was substantial.

Since January 1, 2000 until October 31st, 2006 there have been 75 reported car/truck bombing attacks in the world. In a period of only seven years, the number of bombings has exceeded the number of car and truck bombings in the world for the previous two decades combined. The frequency of attacks using car and truck bombs has increased predominantly due to the violence in Iraq, which accounted for 44 of the 75 reported bombings.

CHAPTER 4

THE HOW'S AND WHY'S OF SUICIDE BOMBERS

There seem to be two schools of thought on the subject of whether or not profiles of suicide bombers are possible. There is the school that believes that profiles are not possible as a profile would indicate the ability to predict and possibly prevent suicide bombers. On the other hand, there is a second school that believes that through the use of psychological autopsies and interviews, a profile of a previous suicide bomber may be determined. Why would this be important? If researchers are able to study what has caused an individual to become a suicide bomber, ante mortem, then it may be possible to see similarities and patterns of individuals sharing common characteristics, thus using those characteristics as a preventive tool.

Profiling Suicide Bombers

Traditionally, researchers have argued that many suicide bombers do not exhibit the signs of suicidal behavior. Lester, Yang, and Lindsay (2004) have studied this opinion in depth and have concluded that both identifying suicidal risk factors as well as preparing a psychological profile are both possible.

Profiling a suicide bomber is a lot like profiling a serial killer except that many serial killers are still alive after their acts have been concluded. If a suicide bomber is successful in their mission, interviewing them is not a possibility.

How do researchers overcome this obstacle? Usually researchers construct a detailed case history about the individual's life and their upbringing. Weisman and Kastenbaum (1968) detailed the proper technique of a psychological autopsy. The psychological autopsy involves reconstructing the life of a completed suicide from their birth until the date of their death. They play emphasis on recent events, moods, statements, and stressors. Utilizing a structured interview procedure, friends, colleagues, lovers, and other individuals in the suicide's life can be interviewed for an insight into their lives. As of 2004, a psychological autopsy has yet to be published related to a suicide bombing incident.

When looking at the socio-demographics of bombers, it would be easy for a researcher to attribute the need to become a suicide bomber with a higher poverty level. As has been previously discussed in this paper, this is not always the case. Schbley (2000) noted that religious martyrs rarely come from wealthy social classes. While this may be the case with some religious martyrs, a case can be made that Palestinian suicide bombers do not conform to this pattern.

Supporting the proven suicide bomber connection, Nolan (1996) issued a report on thirteen suicide bombers between 1994 and 1996. These bombers were found to be unmarried men, ages nineteen to twenty-five from devout Muslim families. They were often middle children in larger families, with only a high school education and they are students in Islamic Fundamentalist Education Centers. Many of these bombers have lived in one of numerous refugee camps and have had a close relative killed in the Intifada.[19] These bombers had a strong Palestinian identity and a sense of hopelessness due to their inability to find work and not enough money to become better educated. Their act will usually result in monetary payments to the family, as previously discussed, as well as the potential scholarships for their siblings to increase their education.

Nolan's report looked at strictly Palestinian suicide bombers, and is not able to be generalized across the globe. Sprinzak (2000) noted that the Sri Lankan Black Tigers are usually split equally between men and women derived from the toughest combat battalions. The suicide bombers from Turkey's Kurdistan Worker's Party are opposite of the Palestinian's as they are mostly young unmarried women ages seventeen to twenty-seven with no professional skills from a large family which has most likely suffered a loss of a relative at the hands of the Turkish Government during the Kurdish struggle.

Lately, Nolan's findings have been changing in that the September 11th terrorists have were older than Nolan's age range, and recently older men as well as younger women have been taking on the roll of a suicide bomber. In Sri Lanka, female suicide bombers are common and it is noted that in the Middle East, there is a rise in the participation of children as well as the middle-aged and married, many of which have children of their own.

---

[19] Intifada- is an Arabic term for "uprising"

Organizational Aspects

Another aspect to consider when dealing with the profiling of suicide bombers is that of an organizational aspect. Very rarely will a suicide bomber be able to plan, prepare, and execute an attack against a significant target without having some type of assistance and possibly mentoring. Moghadam (2003) illustrates the Two-Phase Model of Suicide Bombings. This model considers both the individualized aspects of the bombing, such as the motivations behind the candidates desire to become a human bomb and the organizational aspects, such as the goals and the methods of training and equipping potential bombers.

Individuals lack the ability to properly prepare, plan and execute the objective, while organizations lack the ability to provide a sufficient number of candidates. Most organizations "outsource" for lack of a better word, hence obtaining recruits from another area outside of the organization.

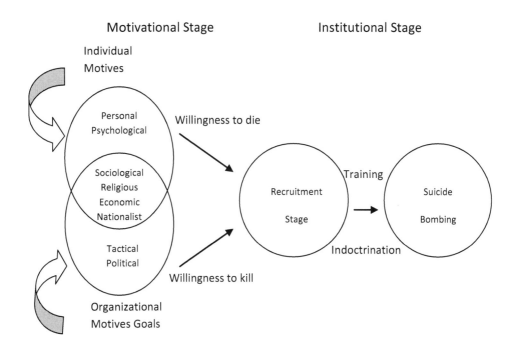

Individual
Motives

Personal
Psychological   Willingness to die

Sociological
Religious   Training
Economic   Recruitment   Suicide
Nationalist

Tactical   Stage   Bombing
Political

Willingness to kill   Indoctrination

Organizational
Motives Goals

Figure 2. The Two-Phase Model (adapted from Moghadam, 2003)

Another thought to consider is the origin of the recruit. It is much easier to

convince an individual to strike against those that they deem have attacked them.

This allows the recruiters to use a pre-determined hatred towards another group to

their advantage. As seen in Figures 3 and 4, the origin of the attacker and the target

region are often opposites.

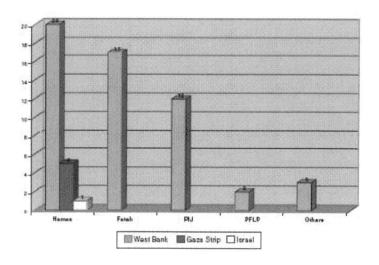

Figure 3. Origin of Attacker by organization, Oct. 2000-June 2002.

(Retrieved from *Studies in Conflict and Terrorism, 26:81, 2003*)

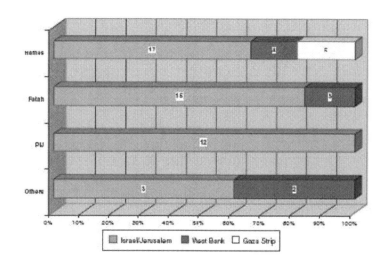

Figure 4. Target Region by organization Oct. 2000- June 2002.

(Retrieved from *Studies in Conflict and Terrorism, 26:68, 2003*)

While Hamas recruited 20 bombers from the West Bank, 17 of their targets were in Israel and Jerusalem. What is even more interesting is that 90% of the recruit bombers were from the West Bank, between October 2000 and June 2002.

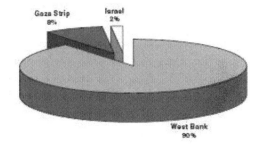

Figure 5 Origin of Attacker, Oct 2000-June 2002

(Retrieved from *Studies in Conflict and Terrorism, 26:86, 2003*)

Moghadam (2003) illustrates the process by which a candidate is recruited and ultimately trained to become a suicide bomber. Candidates are hand picked by their recruiters, most often times volunteers for the assignments are rejected. Hamas[20] and PIJ[21] recruiters have stated that they reject any candidate that may be depressed, as in order to be a martyr bomber, one must want to live. Training and indoctrination may take several weeks to months. The candidates are exposed to propaganda as well as religious teachings to enforce the goal of the organization. Candidates are given several tasks to complete in order to ensure their loyalty and silence. They undergo spiritual cleansing, atonement for their sins and paying off of their debts. Shortly before an assignment, the candidate will disappear from their

---

[20] Hamas- Islamic Resistance Movement, a Palestinian Sunni Islamist organization

[21] PIJ-Palestinian Islamic Jihad Movement-a militant Palestinian group that is designated as a terrorist group Their goal is the liberation of all Palestine, destruction of the State of Israel and its replacement with a state for Palestinians

home without a trace, undergo intensive training in the use of the device assigned for the operation and will prepare their last will and testament. These wills are often used as recruiting propaganda after the death of a successful suicide bomber. Moghadam (2003) further explains that the motivations behind these bombers are usually mixed and that there is no one single motivation associated with the desire to become a bomber. The most common motivations include religion, nationalism, and potential benefits after death. Without a single motivation, stopping these suicide terrorists is a difficult concept. Combined with the organizational aspects of suicide bombings, the current strategies of stopping individual bombers and attempting to gather information from them is flawed. Moghadam (2003) states, "A better long-term strategy would consist of a two-tiered approach targeting the organizations on one hand, and attempting to remove the incentives for individual Palestinians to volunteer for suicide missions on the other."

Young (2002) reveals research that shows the causal link between fundamentalism and terrorism from a psychoanalytic perspective. Psychoanalysis has a different opinion on the nature of suicide bombers than the preceding research in that the individual are inherently damaged and thus their actions are a result of that damage. In order to profile suicide bombers from this perspective, detailed biographies going back to their date of birth and moving forward, with details about every event in their life must be obtained, which would be next to impossible. Hence the reasoning behind why psychological autopsies are as difficult to perform, if not impossible to perform on suicide bombers.

Female Suicide Bombers

This type of profile falls to pieces when dealing with female suicide bombers. Schweitzer (2000) examines the use of female suicide bombers and the frequency of attacks by female bombers. Schweitzer says, "The reasons for using women in particular in this kind of operation evolved from a variety of considerations on the part of the organizations. However, all of them, deceptively used the innocent appearance of a "pregnant" woman in order to by-pass the heavy security arrangements while approaching their targets.

All of them dwell on women's desire to prove their abilities and devotion to the organization and to their supreme leader." In many cultures, woman are viewed as the gentler sex and subject to protection by males and not subjected to such scrutiny. As a result of this belief, female suicide bombers have become a very valuable asset to terrorist groups operating abroad.

It is noted by Zedalis (2004), that the success of suicide bombers depends upon an element of surprise, as well as accessibility to targeted areas or populations. Both of these required elements have been enjoyed by women suicide bombers. The use of female suicide bombers has been in existence for over twenty years. The first reported female suicide bombing attack was in 1985, when a sixteen year old girl drove a truck into an Israeli Defense Force convoy, killing two soldiers (Zedalis 2004). Female suicide bombers have been seen in many theaters and areas of operation. Females have been used in Lebanon, Sri Lanka, Chechnya, Israel and Turkey. Since that time, the LTTE[22] has used women in 30-40% of its bombings which are rumored to have been near 200. While the LTTE may have the highest percentage of female suicide bombers, the Chechen rebels have the notoriety for the highest body count. During a hostage taking at the Theater Center in Chechnya, 170 people were killed in a botched rescue mission. This included 41 rebels and 129 captives.

Interestingly enough in June 1996, the first apparently pregnant female suicide bombing occurred.

This attack was perpetrated by the PKK.[23] In January 2002, the first female martyr in Israel was Wafa Idris. Idris detonated a bomb strapped to her chest, killing one and injuring more than 100 people. She was linked to the Al Aqsa Martyr's Brigade[24]. She was also a Paramedic.   Another interesting first

---

[22] LTTE-Liberation Tigers of Tamil Eelam- also known as the **Tamil Tigers**, is a politico-military organization that has been waging a secessionist campaign against the Sri Lankan government since the 1970s in order to secure a separate state for the Tamil majority regions in the north and east of Sri Lanka

[23] PKK-*Partiya Karkerên Kurdistan* (Kurdistan Worker's Party) an armed militant group, whose stated aim is to create an independent Kurdish state in a territory (sometimes referred to as Kurdistan) that consists of parts of south-eastern Turkey, north-eastern Iraq, north-eastern Syria and north-western Iran.

[24] Al Aqsa Martyr's Brigade- a Palestinian militant group closely linked to the Fatah political party and one of the most active forces in the al-Aqsa Intifada.

bomber, relating back to the notion of Parental Investment and Altruism is Reem al-Reyashi, a 22 year old mother who detonated a bomb at a checkpoint in Israel on January 14th, 2004. She was married with a three year old son and a one year old daughter.

Zedalis points out the reasoning behind using Female suicide bombers. Tactical Advantage as in a stealthier attack, element of surprise, hesitancy to search women and the non-violent stereotype of women, combined with the increased number of available combatants, the publicity that will be received by the "sending" group which in turn will yield a higher number of recruits and the overall psychological effect of using women to deliver a bomb. As with male suicide bombers, the motivations behind a female suicide bomber have yet to be studied in depth enough to make a decision relating to why they would decide to become a bomber. The only evidence that seems to be presented is that the age range is very young, typically 21-23 years old coming from a variety of backgrounds, religious, ethnic, cultural, educational and socioeconomic, just as male suicide bombers do. Many have experienced a loss of a close friend or family member, similar to the recruitment of male Palestinian bombers.

The only question that seems to be presenting an answer is when to recruit female suicide bombers? The LTTE believed bombers should be recruited as young as possible, preadolescent to control their minds and influence their behavior. Russian leaders believe that in order to control a female bomber, they would need complete control over their conditioning, thus recruiting them as young as 11 or 12. (Zedalis 2004) As with male bombers, the motivations behind female suicide bombers are neither clear, nor well studied and this lack of information can ultimately prove to be a determent in the war on Terror.

Psychopathology of Suicide Bombers

Most discussions about suicide bombers as individuals fail to analyze the psychodynamic properties of the act itself. A majority of the discussions mention the charisma of the leadership, the social structure of the group itself, the perceived irrationality of their beliefs, namely in regard to their perceived afterlife and the rewards system that is said to exist, and the potential brainwashing that may have occurred in order to convince a relatively stable individual to commit this act. The major focus in this type of study is on the person's childhood, their adolescence, and social activities that have resulted in an individual being vulnerable and therefore susceptible to the charisma of a strong leader or the structure of the group.

While most individuals who become suicide bombers do not exhibit the traditional warning signs of suicide, they often exhibit the behavioral patterns associated with individuals that join cults. These characteristics include being young with little to no responsibility, not successful in education or work and typically with low self-esteem. These applicants look for a sense of belonging and acceptance and have their failures and frustrations turned into glory and victory.

O'Rourke & Tennant (2005) reviewed studies that most terrorists experience Borderline Personality Disorder in that they are torn between the many roles that they have. However, this has not been the case in a majority of the interviewees. Note, this applies to terrorists in particular and not to suicide bombers, because unless they failed their mission, they are not able to be interviewed. There is no direct correlation between terrorism and mental illness. There does not appear to be a single personality type that fits all terrorists and as such, profiling terrorists and preventing events from occurring has been very difficult. O'Rourke &Tennant (2005) found that their profile results are comparable to that of other researchers in terms of age, education levels, religious background, family and marital status, and place of birth.

Sageman (2004) a psychiatrist by training, analyzed the information presented at the trials for those involved in the 1998 embassy bombings and other data sources to put together a matrix of four hundred terrorists. Of the four hundred biographies reviewed, only four of the men had any slight semblance of mental instability or illness. The only key difference that Sageman found in his research is that the most common method of joining a terrorist cell was to be studying abroad in a country other than your home country, and the target country was neither of the previous two. For example, if you were a Muslim male college student, who was studying in London, England it would be relatively easy to recruit you to attack the United States versus being able to recruit you to attack your hometown.

Hoffman (2002) looks at the mentality of suicide bombers and the use of suicide terrorism and attacks as a psychological warfare agent, especially post September 11th, 2001. "It is, however, important to note that terrorism is designed, as it has always been, to have profound psychological repercussions on a target audience. Fear and intimidation are precisely the terrorists' timeless stock-in-trade. Significantly, terrorism is also designed to undermine confidence in government and leadership (Hoffman, 2002)." While searching for an answer as to how we would end the war on terrorism and eliminate terrorism as a whole, Hoffman (2002) said, "The struggle against terrorism, however, is never-ending. Terrorism has existed for 2,000 years and owes its survival to an ability to adapt and adjust to challenges and countermeasures and to continue to identify and exploit its opponent's vulnerabilities. For success against terrorism, efforts must be as tireless, innovative, and dynamic as that of the opponent." Tireless, innovative and dynamic are terms that can be used to describe suicide bombers, but are not often associated with those individuals suffering or diagnosed with a mental disorder or a psychological pathology.

Madsen (2004) reflects this view in the statement, "Our enemy possesses the most sophisticated weapons in the world and its army is trained to a very high standard. We have nothing with which to repel the killing and thuggery against us except the weapon of martyrdom. It is easy and costs us only our lives: human bombs cannot be defeated, not even by nuclear bombs."

In order to understand the pathology of a suicide bomber, one must understand their logic. Hoffman & McCormick (2004) explain that the role of the suicide bomber is rapidly evolving. Not only is the bomber the primary weapon in an attack, but they are often times the means to a strategic goal. It was stated that "The resort to suicide operations has significantly less to do with the presumed anger, desperation, or frustration of those who actually carry out these attacks, than the strategic requirements of the organizations that send the bombers on their way." The use of suicide bombers as a weapon is much like the use of a conventional weapon, such as a rifle in a war. The bombers simply become a means by which to achieve a goal, more often more dangerous than any rifle on the battlefield.

Pape (2002) illustrates the strategic logic of suicide terrorism from multiple perspectives. Pape has established that there are social and psychological views concerning suicide bombings. Pape argues that the goal of most suicide bombings is "to compel modern democracies to withdraw military forces from territory that the terrorists consider to be their homeland." This is contradictory to the previously explained research about psychological warfare. Pape's suggestion on a victory is that the United States should establish a set of definitive objectives that are easily measurable. These objectives should include "defeating the current pool of terrorists" and "preventing a new generation from arising." Sad to say, but those objectives are easier said than done.

Without a definitive amount of information pertaining to the life of a suicide bomber, psychological autopsies are not possible. The ability to profile suicide bombers take into account many factors, how accurate these profiles will be, and how useful they may be to the government and other agencies associated with Counter Terrorism is in reality, the flip of a coin. If research allows us to accurately predict and profile suicide bombers, this will become an invaluable resource for information. If through our research and experiences, we are not able to predict who a potential bomber might be, we are right back to the proverbial square one. With the continuation of suicide attacks, and the potential failures that may occur, the motivations behind bombings and bombers alike will be able to be studied in greater detail. The only bit of information that appears to be consistent is that a majority of the suicide bombers do not have any type of psychological disturbances, it is merely that they believe strongly in what they are doing, not that they are "crazy."

CHAPTER 5

CONCLUSIONS AND IMPLICATIONS FOR PSYCHOLOGY AND BEHAVIORAL SCIENCES

In order to understand Memetics, the history of memetics and its predecessor must be understood. Originally, Darwin produced evidence that species originated through evolution, and he proposed the theory of natural selection which is the mechanism by which such change occurs. Natural selection is now considered one of the major components of biology. In the 1940's, Ernest Mayr a biologist, worked towards a modern view on Darwinian evolution. His new definition of species allowed for an explanation of how genetic drift occurs and revealed the onset of sub-species. He showed that the most significant reorganization occurred in very small populations cut off from the outside world.

William D. Hamilton, an evolutionary biologist, contributed to the advent of memes with his work in kin selection and his gene-centric view of evolution. Following closely in his footsteps was Robert Trivers, also an evolutionary biologist and a student of Ernest Mayr. Triver's work entailed reciprocal altruism, parental investment, and parent-offspring conflict.

The father of modern memetics was Richard Dawkins. An evolutionary biologist and ethologist, Dawkins wrote *The Selfish Gene* in 1976 which illuminated Hamilton's theory of gene-centric evolution and Dawkins introduced the term, Meme, helping to create the field of memetics. Memetics is simply the study of memes[25]. Memes are a unit of information in the brain that is a mutating replication method in cultural evolution which is contagious and self-propagating. Examples include theme songs, tunes, and catch-phrases. Memes in cultural evolution are similar to genes in genetics.

A group of memes combine to form co-adapted memeplexes or meme complexes. Memes evolve much like other living organisms, that is via natural selection. This allows for competition, inheritance, variation & mutation which modifies their ability to replicate successfully. _The Meme Machine,_ Blackmore (1999) attempted to place memes at the center of a radical and counter intuitive naturalistic theory of mind and personal identity. Her prediction, on the role played by imitation as the cultural replicator and the brain structures that are unique to humans, has been confirmed through research into mirror neurons and the differences in these structures between humans and apes. These neurons allow for flexibility in copying objects for apes, Human beings do not have this ability. Human beings copy exactly, "We see, We do." Mirror neurons are also responsible in part for language acquisition through replication and imitation. Therefore, brain replication is crucial to the cultural evolution of memes.

Memetics, the study of memes, is a controversial field. It offers maximum explanatory value for cases in which other cultural explanations are often

---

[25] Meme-a unit of cultural information that can be transmitted from one mind to another. Coined by Richard Dawkins in 1976. Shortening of the Greek word "mimeme" meaning something imitated.

lacking. Memetics is utilized to explain value judgments, preferences, superstitions, and other unverifiable beliefs.

Memes are replicators and units of information, variation and selection which will ultimately yield new memes. Only some of the variations will survive, as in genetics, therefore showing that memes and selection in human culture will evolve.

Memetic drift[26] increases when meme transmission occurs in an unusual way. This allows for memetic inertia,[27] when the meme transfers along with other devices, i.e. rhymes, tunes, and catch phrases to preserve the memory of the meme prior to transmission. The telephone game[28] is an example of memetic drift.

In terms of suicide terrorism, the liberal interpretation of the Holy Qur'an by recruiters can be seen as memetic drift as the interpretation that the recruiters prefer the candidates to see, will be the meme that the candidates ultimately pass on to others prior to their demise. This replication allows for the survival of the meme.

Religion as a whole is a meme, and studied by memetics. Evangelical

---

[26] Memetic drift-the process of a meme changing as it replicates between one person to another.

[27] Memetic inertia-the characteristic of a meme to manifest in the same way and to have the same impact regardless of who receives or transmits the meme.

[28] Telephone Game-a game often played by children at parties or in the playground in which a phrase or sentence is passed on from one player to another, but is subtly altered in transit.

religious movements are very much memeplexes. As the meme continues to replicate, the meme provides some benefit to its members through a sense of salvation, happiness, and a method to prevent the fear of death. The major religions, Christianity, Islam, and Judaism all developed through the processes of variation, modification and memetic recombination.

Memetic Engineering[29] is responsible for creating and developing theories based on studies of societies and their methods of thinking along with the evolution of their minds. It is based upon mathematico-linguistic analyses of cultural evolution, similar to the level of population genetics.

Role of Memetics in Terrorism

Marsden (2001) points out a valid concern. While the area is still relatively new, contagion psychology lends its hand to the explanation of suicide bombings mainly through a copycat methodology. His research shows that the amount of media coverage devoted to these events, by television networks and newspapers, correlates positively with the rise in subsequent `copycat' events. Marsden gives several good suggestions about how to reduce the copycat effect of suicide attacks.

---

[29] Memetic engineering-is the process of developing memes through meme splicing and meme synthesis with the intent of altering the behavior of others.

1. Avoid presenting the event as an accomplishment; for example, do not use the term 'successful'

2. Avoid repetitious or excessive reporting of the event

3. Avoid sensationalizing the event

4. Avoid `how-to' descriptions of the event

5. Avoid portraying the event as painless for those responsible

6. Avoid presenting simplistic explanations for the event

7. Avoid glorifying the event or those responsible for it

8. Avoid giving a positive rationale for those responsible for the event

By utilizing these suggestions, it is Marsden's hope that the volume of suicide bombings will decrease through the lack of recognition and the impact on the general public in their attempt to spread their psychological distress.

In particular, suggestion two: Avoid repetitious or excessive reporting of the event. If this had been used in conjunction with the media coverage of the events of September 11th , it would have reduced the impact of the event for many people. How many times did any given person watch the towers burning and falling on TV? How many individuals were unable to sleep that night as a result of the continued news media coverage of the event and the worries connected with the World Trade Center? The psychological damage was done, partially due to the terrorist attack, and secondarily due to the media's repeated coverage of the attacks.

This is an example of where social engineering[30] would play a huge role. If the news media, were to discontinue publicizing the actions of terrorists, and in particular suicide bombers, there may be less of an attempt to continue utilizing these tactics if the desired message of the bomber will not be carried on after their death. If the media were to utilize social engineering, and rename suicide bombings, with their allure and fascination, into homicide bombings would this bring about a change in the nature of the event? Would an individual bomber, looking to become a martyr and ending their life willfully continue with their mission and their overall objective if they were not going to be considered suicide bombers? Looking back at the events of September 11th , 2001 the overall media

---

[30] Social engineering- a concept in political science that refers to efforts to influence popular attitudes and social behavior on a large scale, whether by governments or private groups.

coverage produced through this suicide attack was phenomenal. Nacos (2003) analyzes the attacks of September 11th, 2001 in terms of being a 'successful' suicide attack. and as such, the allure to attempt another attack of this same magnitude. Schweitzer (2000) predicted, whether knowingly or unknowingly, a large-scale incident. "The greatest potential risk suicide terrorism may pose in the future is if terrorists carry out operations combined with other spectacular tactics such as blowing up airplanes or the use of Weapons of Mass Destruction. Such a combination will increase immensely the death toll of a single terror attack and will have a shocking psychological effect on public morale. At this level suicide terrorism would constitute a genuine strategic threat and would probably be confronted as such." That statement was made eighteen months before the September 11th attacks.

Nacos shows how the events of 9/11/01 contributed to the overall goals of the terrorists as they increased media and news coverage, which according to Marsden (2001) needs to be contained, as well as achieved their immediate and near term goals. Nacos (2003) states, "Although the possibility of terrorists getting hold of and using weapons of mass destruction some day cannot be ignored, the more immediate concern must be the prospect that 9-11, in one form or another, might well become the most attractive model for terrorism in the near future."

Nacos illustrates the saying, "He who does not learn from the past, is doomed to repeat it." Our failure to learn from the events of September 11th, 2001 will ultimately lead to more successful attacks of a greater magnitude. The ability of the media to sensationalize a terrorist event may well lead to the promulgation of another event of a similar if not larger caliber.

Memetic Engineering as described by Pech (2003) fits in with Marsden's notion that some terrorism is a result of copying behavior. An individual's ability to replicate the negative behavior of suicide bombings can potentially be curtailed if the replication is understood and modified. If these acts are labeled as undesirable, then the act loses its value and has less desirable outcomes to the receiver. A few examples of this might be the Oklahoma City Coward instead of the Oklahoma City Bomber, and the Washington Weakling for the D.C. Snipers (Pech 2003).

Franzoi (1996) points out that copying behavior have been seen in the past in relation to the famous murders of Jack the Ripper in 1888, and the eight copycat murders that occurred with a year of those murders. Franzoi points out that there are three possible explanations can be drawn about copying behavior. The first is disinhibition, which states that people viewing other people's violent acts reduces an individuals inhibition to commit the same act. Secondly, the formation of aggressive scripts can develop in individuals viewing violent acts. An aggressive script is a preconception of how an event is supposed to occur. Finally there is cognitive priming, which suggests that objects associated with violence may create thoughts and behaviors towards acts of violence.

So what about terrorism makes people want to commit these types of acts? The answer might be in social learning. Part of social learning is the ability to copy the behaviors of individuals that we admire and actions that we considerable desirable. This is where the terrorist meme can come into play.

Terrorist Meme

Is there such a thing as the terrorist meme? Is there a self-propagating idea that encourages the candidate to commit an act of terrorism? There seems to be a certain amount of contagion and propagation associated with terrorism. Social learning is based on imitation, suggesting that a suicide bomber candidate views the violent acts of another suicide bomber; acts which can be considered admirable and worthy of imitation. This is also a terrorist meme. This terrorism meme needs to be copied in order to ensure its survival. Copying and replicating this meme in increasing numbers ensures its own survivability, much akin to Darwin's survival of the fittest, given a proper memetic environment.

According to Pech (2003), "The memes of violence in the form of terrorism have found the ideal vehicle for replication in the media." Terroristic acts have a certain degree of shock and awe to the general public. As such, the general public feels the need to be informed about incidents of terrorism therefore creating an environment where terrorism sells. This allows for the replication of the terrorist meme, through repeated exposure to the news headlines, graphic images, and sound clips of Terroristic acts. The prime example of this in recent history has been the September 11th attacks. In the aftermath of the attacks, numerous news channels around the globe were showing the images of jet liners flying into the towers, the resulting fires that consumed the structural steel, and ultimately the collapse of both the North and South Tower. These images when viewed by possible candidates of a terrorist organization allow for the propagation of the terrorist meme, viewing the "big win" in their war against the Infidels. These images would act as encouragement to other potential terrorists that attacks of this magnitude are not only possible, but incredibly detrimental to the intended victim or group.

Pech (2003) said, "The key to reducing the incidence of terrorism would then lied in the elimination of such a meme." But how do we as a society contribute to the extinction of a meme? Having the news media change their reporting style would be an option however this would not be very prudent as the media, like most organizations is resistant to change. The second option would to be fully understand the meme in order to provide for its extinction. What information does the meme contain and how does the meme typically replicate? The information contained in the terrorist meme which contributes to the behavior of the potential terrorist could be modified and/or removed from the meme itself. The flowchart shows how the modification of a meme can occur.

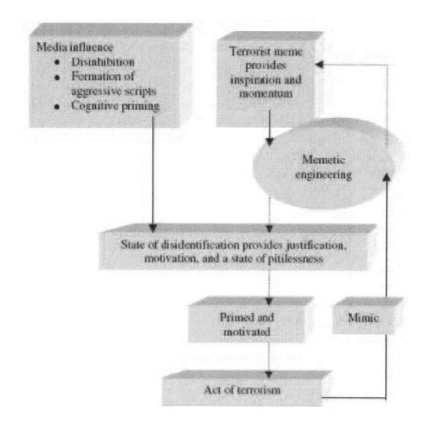

Figure 6. Memetic Engineering and Inhibiting Terrorism

(Retrieved from *Journal of Contingencies and Crisis Management*, **11,** p.65) Memetic Engineering offers much in terms of a plausible explanation of terrorism as well as a means of redress for Terrorism.

However, the best way to address the terrorist meme, isn't through extinction. If society were able to engineer a newer, better meme that would be more successful in its replication and infectious capabilities, it would be able to replace the terrorist meme, therefore reducing the potential spread of terrorism. Constructing this meme is a somewhat difficult concept to tackle.

Memes and Culture

Understanding how memes work, or how they replicate has lead researchers to a better understanding of culture as a whole. According to Aunger (2003), Culture is a product of human intelligence, and it is only a product of the human mind. Memes and their influence on culture therefore, are only in the mind. Blackmore (1999) shows how we stick to defining the meme as it has been passed on, mostly through imitation and the status presented by the aggressor who is being imitated.

Culture is also a product of evolution. Being culture is in the mind, evolution may place a role in the manipulation of memes and the destruction of unhealthy memes, while allowing for the preservation of "good" memes. The terrorist meme, as previously discussed, through evolution may be destroyed or modified so that it does not replicate in the current fashion. If the meme were to be modified, the rewards associated with imitating the act itself would not be as relevant, and the potential status associated would be denied.

Therefore, through culture and evolution, the act of suicide terrorism with help from memes may ultimately be ended. The use of memes to examine evolution and culture along with the ability to manipulate memes through memetic engineering and drift, would allow researchers to understand the desire to be a suicide bomber, while increasing the imitation of a positive meme such as one of tolerance, or the ability to work together to resolve problems.

In conclusion, the idea of suicide bombers is relatively new having only been present for under a hundred years. However, the idea of utilizing human beings as weapons to influence policy, create change, and win wars is not a new concept. Through the understanding of the rewards of the recruited suicide bomber, researchers can modify their strategy to successfully deal with, and mitigate the problem of suicide bombers. This will not be an easy task by any means.

GLOSSARY

Al Aqsa Martyr's Brigade: a Palestinian militant group closely linked to theFatah political party and one of the most active forces in the al-Aqsa Intifada

Al-Bukhari: an Arabic nesbat, meaning "from Bukhara", the old Persian location of what is today Uzbekistan. It is usually added at the end of names as a specifier. The most known Al-Bukhari is Muhammad Ibn Ismail al-Bukhari, the Sunni scholar.

Altruism: The practice of placing others before oneself

Asymmetric Warfare: a term that describes a military situation in which two belligerents of unequal strength interact and take advantage of theirrespective strengths and weaknesses. This interaction often involves strategies and tactics outside the bounds of conventional warfare.

Black Tiger Unit: special operatives of the LTTE that commit suicide ifneeded to reach their objectives. They are considered to be one of the mostelite and lethal suicide bombers in the world.

Hadith: traditions relating to the words and deeds of Muhammad. Hadithcollections are regarded as important tools for determining the Sunnah, or Muslim way of life, by all traditional schools of jurisprudence.

Hamas: Islamic Resistance Movement, a Palestinian Sunni Islamist organization

Inclusive Fitness (IF): encompasses conventional Darwinian fitness with the addition of behaviors that contribute to an organism's individual fitness through altruism. An organism's ultimate goal is to leave the maximum number of viable offspring possible, thereby keeping their genes present within a population.

Infidel: one who doubts or rejects central tenets of a religion, especially those regarding its deities. One who doubts or rejects a particular doctrine, system orprinciple. In Islam, the Arabic word *kafir* refers to non-Muslims, often in a derogatory sense, and is usually translated into English as "infidel" or "unbeliever".

Intifada: is an Arabic term for "uprising"

IRA: Irish Republican Army

Islamic Dawa Party: Islamic Call Party is a militant Shiite Islamic group.

Jihad: is often used to describe purely physical and military "religious war",through physical struggle. Muslim scholars say that this understanding only makes up part of the broader meaning of the concept of *jihad*. The denotation is of a struggle, challenge, difficulty or (frequently) opposed effort, made either in accomplishment or as resistance.

Kaiten: one or two man piloted torpedoes.

LTTE: Liberation Tigers of Tamil Eelam- also known as the Tamil Tigers, is a politico-military organization that has been waging a secessionist campaign against the Sri Lankan government since the 1970s in order to secure a separate state for the Tamil majority regions in the north and east of Sri Lanka

Malik: Anas ibn Malik ibn al-Nadr (d.ca. 709) was a well-known *sahabi* (companion) of the Prophet Muhammad. He had been presented to the Muhammad by his mother at an early age in fulfillment of a vow. After the Muhammad's death in 632 he participated in the wars of conquest. One hundred and twenty eight *ahadith* narrated on his authority are to be found in the collections of *Sahih Bukhari* and *Sahih Muslim*.

Meme: a unit of cultural information that can be transmitted from one mind to another.Coined by Richard Dawkins in 1976. Shortening of the Greek word "mimeme" meaning something imitated.

Memetic drift: the process of a meme changing as it replicates between one person to another.

Memetic engineering: the process of developing memes through memesplicing and meme synthesis with the intent of altering the behavior of others.

Memetic inertia: the characteristic of a meme to manifest in the same way and to have the same impact regardless of who receives or transmits the meme.

Mu'min: Believing Muslim

Parental investment (PI): refers to a concept in evolutionary ecology defined as any parental expenditure (time, energy etc.) that benefits one offspring at a cost to parents' ability to invest in other components of fitness. Components of fitness include the wellbeing of existing offspring, parents' future reproduction, and inclusive fitness through aid to kin.

PIJ: Palestinian Islamic Jihad Movement-a militant Palestinian group that is designated as a terrorist group Their goal is the liberation of all Palestine, destruction of the State of Israel and its replacement with a state for Palestinians.

PKK: *Partiya Karkerên Kurdistan* (Kurdistan Worker's Party) an armed militant group, whose stated aim is to create an independent Kurdish state in aterritory (sometimes referred to as Kurdistan) that consists of parts of southeastern Turkey, north-eastern Iraq, north-eastern Syria and north-western Iran.

Shaheed Mujahid: Shaheed is a religious term in Islam, that literally means "witness". It is a title that is given to a Muslim after his death, if he died during fulfillment of a religious commandment, or during a war for the religion. After fulfilling their religious commandment, a Muslim is to receive 72 red headed virgins in heaven. Mujahid- is an Arabic term, literally translated means "struggler"

Shari'ah: refers to the body of Islamic law. The term means "way" or "path"; it is the legal framework within which public and some private aspects of life are regulated for those living in a legal system based on Muslim principles of jurisprudence

Social engineering: a concept in political science that refers to efforts to influence popular attitudes and social behavior on a large scale, whether by governments or private groups.

Telephone Game: a game often played by children at parties or in the playground in which a phrase or sentence is passed on from one player to another, but is subtly altered in transit.

TNT: an explosive with the common designation *trinitrotoluene*. The explosive yield of TNT is considered the standard measure of strength of bombs and other explosives

Total Fertility Rate (TFR): The average number of children that would be born to a woman over her lifetime if she were to experience the current age-specific fertility rates through her lifetime.

REFERENCES

Atran, S. (2003) Genesis of suicide terrorism. *Science, 299,* 5612.

Aunger, R. (2003) *Darwinizing Culture.* Oxford: Oxford University Press

Blackmore, S. (2000) *The Meme Machine.* Oxford: Oxford University Press

Blackwell, A. (2005) *Terrorism, Heroism, and Altruism. Kin Selection and socio-religious cost-benefit scaling in Palestinian suicide attack.* Oregon: University of Oregon

Bloom, M. (2004) *Dying to kill: The global phenomenon of suicide terror.* New York: Columbia University Press.

Dawkins, R. (1976) *The Selfish Gene* Oxford: Oxford University Press.

Franzoi, S. (1996) *Social Psychology,* Dubuque; IA. Brown & Benchmark Publisher.

Hamilton, W. (1964). The genetical evolution of social behaviour I and II. *Journal of Theoretical Biology,* **7,** 1-16 & 17-52.

Hoffman, B. (2002) Rethinking terrorism and counterterrorism since 9/11. *Studies in Conflict & Terrorism, 25,* 303–316.

Hoffman, B., & McCormick, G. (2004) Terrorism, signaling, and suicide attack *Studies in Conflict & Terrorism, 27,* 243–281.

Khashan, H. (2003) Collective Palestinian frustration and suicide bombings *Third World Quarterly, 24,* 6, 1049–1067.

Krueger, A. & Maleckova, J. (2003) Education, Poverty, & Terrorism: Is there a casual connection? *Journal of Economic Perspectives,* 17, 4, 119-144.

Kruglanski, A. & Golec, A. (2004) Individual Motivations, The Group Process and Organizational Strategies in Suicide Terrorism E. Meyersson Milgrom (Ed.) *Suicide Missions and the Market for Martyrs, A Multidisciplinary Approach.* Princeton, N.J.: Princeton University Press

Lester, D., Yang, B., & Lindsay, M. (2004) Suicide Bombers: Are Psychological Profiles Possible? *Studies in Conflict & Terrorism, 27,* 283–295.

Madsen, J. (2004) Suicide Terrorism: Rationalizing the Irrational. *Strategic Insights,* 3, 8.

Marsden, P. (2001) Copycat Terrorism: Fanning the Fire. *Journal of Memetics-Evolutionary Models of Information Transmission.* 5.

Moghadam, A. (2003) Palestinian Suicide Terrorism in the Second Intifada Motivations and Organizational Aspects. *Studies in Conflict & Terrorism,* 26, 65-92.

Mumford, G. (2004) Explosive Growth of Suicide Terrorism Brings Psychological Scientists to the Table. *A Publication of the American Psychological Association Science Directorate* 18.

Nacos, B. (2003) The Terrorist Calculus behind 9-11: A Model for Future Terrorism? *Studies in Conflict & Terrorism,* 26, 1–16.

Nolan, S. (1996) Portrait of a Suicide Bomber. *Independent on Sunday,* 10 March. 13.

O'Rourke, L. & Tennant, N. (2005) *A Sociobiological View of Palestinian Suicide Bombers.* Ohio State University, Ohio.

Pape, R. (2005) *Dying to Win: The Strategic Logic of Suicide Terrorism,* Random House, New York.

Pech, R. (2003) Inhibiting Imitative Terrorism through Memetic Engineering. *Journal of Contingencies and Crisis Management,* 11, 61-66.

Ratner, C. (2004) A Cultural Critique of Psychological Explanations of Terrorism. *Cross-Cultural Psychology Bulletin,* 38, 18-24.

Sageman, M. (2004) *Understanding Terror Networks.* University of Pennsylvania Press

Schbley, A. (1990) Religious Terrorists: What They Aren't Going to Tell Us. *Terrorism,* 13. 237-241.

Schbley, A. (2000) Torn between God, Family, and Money. *Studies in Conflict & Terrorism,* 23, 175-196.

Schweitzer, Y. (2000) *Suicide Terrorism: Development & Characteristics.* International Conference on Countering Suicide Terrorism at ICT, Herzeliya, Israel.

Sprinzak, E. (2000) Rational Fanatics. *Foreign Policy*, Sept/Oct., 66-73.

The Hijacked Caravan: Refuting Suicide Bombings as Martyrdom Operations in Contemporary Jihad Strategy. (2000.) Retrieved October 10, 2006 from http://www.ihsanic-intelligence.com/dox/The_Hijacked_Caravan.pdf

Trivers, R. (1972) Parental investment and sexual selection. In B. Campbell (Ed.) *Sexual selection and the descent of man, 1871-1971* (pp. 136-179). Chicago: Aldine.

Weisman, A. & Kastenbaum R. (1968) The Psychological Autopsy. *Community Mental Health Monograph,* 4. New York: Behavioral Publications.

Young, R. (2001) *Psychoanalysis, Terrorism, and Fundamentalism.* London: Process Press

Zedalis, D. (2004) *Female Suicide Bombers*, The Strategic Studies Institute, U.S. Army War College, Carlisle, PA. http://www.carlisle.army.mil/ssi/.

Made in the USA
Lexington, KY
03 June 2011